PEANUT BUTTER, APPLE BUTTER, CINNAMON TOAST

Food Riddles for You to Guess

First Steck-Vaughn Edition 1992

Copyright © 1990 American Teacher Publications

Published by Steck-Vaughn Company

Library of Congress number: 90-8036

Library of Congress Cataloging in Publication Data.

Palacios, Argentina.
  Peanut butter, apple butter, cinnamon toast; food riddles for you to guess / by Argentina Palacios;
illustrated by Ben Mahan.

  (Ready-set-read)
  Summary: Riddles in rhyme describe foods such as spaghetti, popcorn, apples, and carrots.
  1. Riddles—Juvenile literature. 2. Food—Juvenile humor. [1. Food—Wit and humor. 2. Riddles.]
I. Mahan, Ben, ill. II. Title. III. Series.
PN6371.5.P35 818′.5402—dc20   1990   90-8036

ISBN 0-8172-3584-1   hardcover library binding

ISBN 0-8114-6745-7   softcover binding

      4 5 6 7 8 9 0   96 95 94

READY·SET·READ

Peanut Butter, Apple Butter, Cinnamon Toast

Food Riddles for You to Guess

by Argentina Palacios

illustrated by Ben Mahan

RSVP

RAINTREE
STECK-VAUGHN
PUBLISHERS
The Steck-Vaughn Company

Austin, Texas

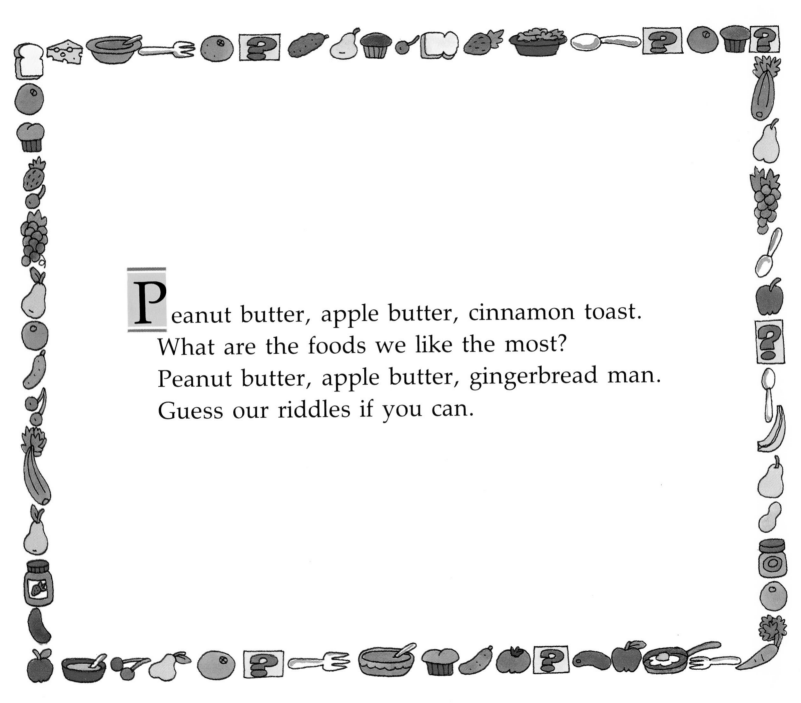

Peanut butter, apple butter, cinnamon toast.
What are the foods we like the most?
Peanut butter, apple butter, gingerbread man.
Guess our riddles if you can.

4

Have some in a cone or cup.
What flavor do you pick?
It's cold. It's sweet. It's melting. . . .
Better eat it quick!

What is it?

Ice cream

Red sauce on white noodles.
Grate on lots of cheese.
Don't you want that meatball?
Pass it to me, please.

What is it?

Spaghetti

Give a red one to your teacher,
Or bake some in a pie.
This fruit can be delicious.
There are many kinds to try.

What is it?

An apple

Without this food, no sandwich
Would ever be complete.
Do you like rye, do you like white,
Or do you like whole wheat?

What is it?

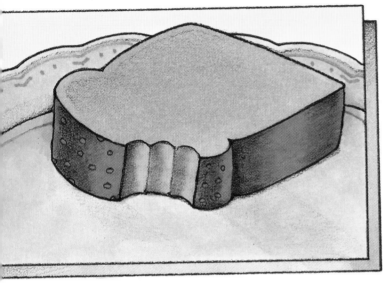

Bread

This vegetable is orange,
And underground it grows.
It's great for stews or salads,
Or for a snowman's nose.

What is it?

A carrot

It's fluffy, white, and crunchy—
A perfect movie treat.
You pop it in a popper,
Then scoop some up to eat.

What is it?

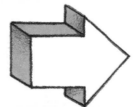

Popcorn

This fruit is long and yellow,
A monkey's favorite meal.
You can eat one anytime,
But first take off the peel.

What is it?

A banana

It's boiled, fried, or scrambled,
And used in baking, too.
But if you drop and break it,
The "yolk" may be on you!

What is it?

An egg

Have it with some jelly
Or by itself on bread.
Creamy smooth or chunky—
Which kind should I spread?

What is it?

Peanut butter

Peanut butter, apple butter, cinnamon toast.
What are the foods YOU like the most?

Sharing the Joy of Reading

Reading a book aloud to your child is just one way you can help your child experience the joy of reading. Now that you and your child have shared **Peanut Butter, Apple Butter, Cinnamon Toast,** you can help your child begin to think and react as a reader by encouraging him or her to:

- Retell or reread the story with you, looking and listening for the repetition of specific letters, sounds, words, or phrases.

- Make a picture of a favorite character, event, or key concept from this book.

- Talk about his or her own ideas and feelings about the subject of this book and other things he or she might want to know about this subject.

Here is an activity that you can do together to help extend your child's appreciation of this book: You and your child can each identify your favorite foods. Together, you might want to make these foods and eat them.